7 Steps for EFFECTIVE COMMUNICATION in your MARRIAGE

MICHAEL & LADY CAROLYN BYRD

Copyright © 2019 Michael & Carolyn Byrd

ISBN: 978-0-9817864-0-7

Byrd Family Books

All rights reserved no part of this book may be reproduced, stored in a retrieval system, or transmitted by any means without the written permission of the authors.

TABLE OF CONTENTS

7 steps to effective communication in your marriage. 1

Sending and Receiving 3

Listening without judgment 6

Know the truth 10

Is it worth an argument? 14

It's okay to disagree but do it with respect 17

Finding the solution 21

Love must be the foundation always 24

7 STEPS TO EFFECTIVE COMMUNICATION IN YOUR MARRIAGE.

Aside from a lack of money, another equally highly destructive element in marriage is a lack of communication, or poor communication. Even the rich get divorced or run into huge problems along these lines. If money were the only consideration as some people make it seem, then the rich shouldn't have problems in their marriages, but we know better than to think that way, so the need for effective communication in marriages can't be overemphasized, but should be thoroughly understood. Here are 7 steps towards enhancing and developing a healthy communication lifestyle between couples.

SENDING AND RECEIVING

It's very common place to hear people say, he doesn't listen or she does not listen, and that is because what is being said is often not being attended to or considered. The art of speaking and listening in communication is one that transcends all forms of relationships. No one wants to be with someone who doesn't listen but the sad truth is, many people seldom listen and this is even truer in marriages. The problem is often misunderstood what it means to listen and often speak destructively because of this.

To listen isn't just a physical exercise of vibrations hitting the eardrum through sound waves. It's genuinely acknowledging and considering what information is being received.

We hear with our ears, but listen with our heart. It is more than just words. True acts of listening involves looking beyond the speaker's words, and in this case, one's partner. It also involves paying attention to things being said and things not being said like tone, body language, actions etc.

We must also form the habit of expressing ourselves well and this is only possible when we learn to listen as well. Proper listening promotes good response and both aids effective communication.

LISTENING WITHOUT JUDGMENT

It can be said that listening is good, but emphasis must be placed on how to listen as well. When we listen, we should not judge. To judge is to condemn one's partner. This is bad for a number of reasons. For one, it kills the entire communication process in the sense that, rather than focus on the solution, it puts the focus on the problem.

Secondly, if one feels condemned every time, they might not be willing to speak anymore. This doesn't mean that corrections aren't in place. It simply means that such corrections should be done with positivity. Let's have a look at a scenario. A man comes home to meet his wife furious and here comes the question, where have you been? To this the man responds, I went out to see some friends. We had things to discuss.

Here are two possible replies;

i. "You went out with your friends leaving me at home, does that make any sense to you, and what reasonable man would do that?"

ii. "I know you want to have some fun, but I also need you and I believe that I am more important to you as your wife. You can always balance both".

Now let's analyze both responses, the reality is that the first response is purely unacceptable and is very judgmental. To the second, he's gone out to talk about a business proposal and at no point did he say he wanted to have some fun. If care isn't taken, things could go out of control real quick. A smart move on the husband's part would be to understand why she said what she said and explain what the real intention was, with love.

It would be unwise for him to go, "What sort of thinking is this, I never said I was going to have fun or get defensive and go, "When you went out last year without telling me, did I complain? Are you so porous in the head?" This might seem extreme but it might surprise you to know that this is how some people respond in a situation such as this.

KNOW THE TRUTH

The most fundamental truth in all of this is that, your partner is a team mate and a team mate is a loved one, your number one. If you can define the position of your partner in your life, it would make things easier. They love you and do not desire to hurt you. This must remain foremost in your thoughts.

It is tempting to look to a partner and expect them to change when it is we that need to change first. We should build a capacity for love that would help us deal with the complexity of living with an imperfect lover. They aren't perfect and can have a tendency to make mistakes at times. This is where the whole situation stems from. It is born out of ignorance, not hatred. This doesn't excuse every, and all misbehaviors but it does provide room for growth. Sometimes it takes time to build communication and it can always get better. We must be patient enough to allow this growth.

This would come in handy with partners that we might term difficult. Let's not forget, communication isn't just what we say but everything, including what we do. It might seem difficult marrying the idea that one's partner loves them and still behave in ways that show the opposite.

It is very possible that what you might perceive as being bad or unacceptable, could otherwise be alright to your partner. This is exactly what communication should solve. It deals with not just the obvious but the trivial things as well, and nothing is trivial if they have a potential for destroying the entire thing as well.

One more thing that comes in play automatically then is trust. It takes trust to get to a place where you can forgive the inevitable on the basis of a positive eventuality. Your partner communicates with you every day, in every way. Listen!

IS IT WORTH AN ARGUMENT?

The desire to be right is a universal one. Everyone wants to be right and it is almost like an urge, but the truth is not only can we not always be right, it is often difficult to know when we are wrong for if we knew we were wrong, perhaps we wouldn't take that position in the first place. There are situations where the concept of right or wrong just doesn't apply. It is also true that we often want people to know when we are right as well.

This stoic attitude of always wanting to be right often leads to problems and must be curtailed. Right or wrong, the most important consideration should be the growth of your marriage. If an argument threatens to destroy the marriage, then it might be very prudent to drop it. It isn't worth it. One could ask him or herself, does the end justify the means? "Is it worth an argument, or should I dismiss my right to be right?"

It should be clear to us now that there is no substitute to a healthy marriage. This should be the goal and effective communication helps in achieving this, not unnecessary arguments.

Finally, we should be able to admit our faults. We should be able to say we are sorry whenever we discover that we are wrong, or when we realize that things are going out of control. The former might be easy but the latter takes maturity and a high level of self-control, isn't that what communication requires anyway.

IT'S OKAY TO DISAGREE BUT DO IT WITH RESPECT

It is unrealistic to expect that two individuals would always think the same way all the time. Not even siblings born on the same day do this. In fact, it is practically impossible. After all, this is what leads to arguments in the first place but it doesn't have to be.

It is expected that partners would disagree, but it should be done with respect.

To respect a partner is to have due regards for the feelings, wishes or rights of that person. It is irrespective of what the bone of contention might be.

We all have differences but it should be an advantage. It ensures that at least to an extent, there would be different angles looking at solutions to problems. Aside from the fact that human beings are different, we also have male and female differences and that is a topic for another day. The important thing is to know that part what it means to be and stay married is the ability to deal with differences daily.

As a man, you should not disregard your wife in a distasteful manner. She could come up with ideas that you might consider unorthodox, but learn to address her as an equal even during conversations. Let her know that you respect her as well.

As a woman, do not see your husband as some senseless zombie. Learn to listen to him and proffer your own unique ideas in a way that he would understand, with respect. Let him see that you value and honor him all the same, even when you don't see eye to eye on a given issue.

The bottom line isn't to expect no tendency for an argument but to learn to manage the situation accordingly.

FINDING THE SOLUTION

There will be challenges during marriage and focus should be on finding solutions, not stressing problems. To which, we see the exact opposite. There is a dangerous culture permeating our society today as regards marriage. It is a culture of divorce. We see it being propagated all over social media as well. Today, people are impatient, materialistic to every extent, greedy, dishonest, and wicked and all sorts. It was always like this but for some unfortunate reasons, it has become this. A reporter once asked an old couple, 65 years in marriage, how they managed to stay together for so long. To this the woman replied, "We were born in a time when if something was broken, we would fix it, not throw it away". This is priceless. Today however, this is often not the case, with divorce at an all-time high, one would wonder what the problem is. We have all sorts of misguided individuals seeking exit from their marriages over issues that could be resolved.

The problem is that couples aren't willing to communicate anymore. Everyone is now chasing everything else but the knowledge required to truly maintain a healthy marriage. It is hard work, absolutely, and that is more reason to keep level heads and communicate with each other.

We must imbibe a solution driven culture and facilitate this using communication.

LOVE MUST BE THE FOUNDATION ALWAYS.

There is a common idea that in marriage, money is all that matters, we completely disagree. Love is all that matters. When we say love, we mean it, not the diluted and often misplaced version we see in the world today. The reason why money often acts like a prima donna is because it is indeed important. It is so important that the Bible calls it a defense. However, to say it is more important than love is often a statement that is made out of ignorance. This belief system that money is above all or money first then the rest can follow is possibly why there is so much a problem today. If the foundation was love, then it would be literally impossible to get to where we are today, for love brings closer, not divide.

Money is a tool but love is life.

Money is relative, but love is absolute.

The reason we have placed money and love side by side is these two are often the biggest topics in marriages and often appear in the same discussion. Both are very needed, but only one can truly serve as a foundation, and it is love, after all God is love. If this doesn't explain it, then nothing else can.

Let's ask ourselves. If money was the solution, why do rich couples divorce? If money was more powerful than love, how much did we pay to win our creator's love?

Love Matters

Give Love, Receive Love

Think Love, Manifest Love

Speak Love, Listen to Love

Show Love, Embrace Love

Let unconditional love be the foundation of your marriage.

www.ingramcontent.com/pod-product-compliance
Lightning Source LLC
Chambersburg PA
CBHW050609300426
44112CB00013B/2137